INSIDE MLB

HOUSTON ASTROS

Sam Rhodes

WORLD SERIES ★ 2017 ★ CHAMPIONS

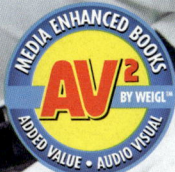

AV² provides enriched content that supplements and complements this book. Weigl's AV² books strive to create inspired learning and engage young minds in a total learning experience.

Your AV² Media Enhanced books come alive with...

Audio
Listen to sections of the book read aloud.

Key Words
Study vocabulary, and complete a matching word activity.

Video
Watch informative video clips.

Quizzes
Test your knowledge.

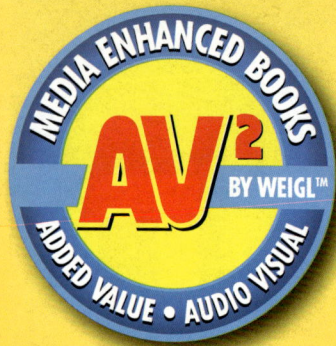

Go to www.av2books.com, and enter this book's unique code.

BOOK CODE

AVE25528

Embedded Weblinks
Gain additional information for research.

Slide Show
View images and captions, and prepare a presentation.

AV² by Weigl brings you media enhanced books that support active learning.

Try This!
Complete activities and hands-on experiments.

... and much, much more!

Published by AV² by Weigl
350 5th Avenue, 59th Floor
New York, NY 10118
Website: www.av2books.com

Library of Congress Control Number: 2017963689

ISBN 978-1-4896-7977-2 (hardcover)
ISBN 978-1-4896-7978-9 (softcover)
ISBN 978-1-4896-7979-6 (multi-user eBook)

Printed in the United States of America in Brainerd, Minnesota
1 2 3 4 5 6 7 8 9 0   22 21 20 19 18

012018
120817

Project Coordinator: John Willis   Designer: Nick Newton

Every reasonable effort has been made to trace ownership and to obtain permission to reprint copyright material. The publishers would be pleased to have any errors or omissions brought to their attention so that they may be corrected in subsequent printings.

The publisher acknowledges Getty Images, Alamy, and iStock as its primary image suppliers for this title.

Contents

Go, Astros! 4

Who Are the Astros? 7

Where They Came From 8

Who They Play 11

Where They Play 12

The Baseball Diamond 15

Big Days 16

Tough Days 19

Meet the Fans 21

Heroes Then... 23

Heroes Now... 24

Gearing Up 27

Sports Stats 28

Quiz 30

Key Words/Index 31

Log on to www.av2books.com 32

GO, ASTROS!

The people of Houston, Texas, know how to overcome challenges. Their baseball team is tough, too. The Houston Astros have not been around as long as many other teams, but they are here to stay. Through hard work, they have become a world-class team. The Astros are training and practicing every day, which paid off in 2017 with their first ever **World Series** win.

The first **World Series** ever played in the state of Texas was at the **Astros'** home field, **Minute Maid Park**, in 2005.

In 2017, the Astros became the only team in history to have five different players hit home runs in a single World Series game.

At 5 feet, 6 inches (168 centimeters) tall, José Altuve is tied for the shortest active player in Major League Baseball.

Who Are the Astros?

Major League Baseball (MLB) consists of the American League (AL) and the National League (NL). Each league has three **divisions**: East, Central, and West. The Houston Astros play in the American League West Division. After the regular season ends, the playoffs start. The best teams in each division, plus two **wild card** teams, make the playoffs. The Astros have made the playoffs 11 times in their **franchise** history.

The **Houston Astros** played in the **National League** from 1962 to 2012, switching to the American League in **2013**.

WHERE THEY CAME FROM

The Houston Astros were not always called the Astros. They started as the Houston Colt .45s in 1962. From 1961 to 1962, the American League and the National League each added two new teams. These four expansion teams would make baseball more competitive. The Colt .45s were one of those teams. Three years later, in 1965, they changed their name to the Houston Astros.

Right fielder Kevin Bass played for the Astros from 1982 to 1989 and then again from 1993 to 1994.

The name Astros is from a word that means "**outer space**." It comes from Houston's connection to the **U.S. Space Program**.

The Astros won more away games than home games in the 2017 regular season. Third baseman Alex Bregman had 84 hits while away and 74 at home.

Who They Play

Every MLB team plays 162 games in a season. Of those games, 76 are played against teams in their division. Other teams in the American League West Division are the Los Angeles Angels, the Seattle Mariners, the Texas Rangers, and the Oakland Athletics. The Texas Rangers are the Astros' biggest **rivals**. When the Astros moved into the same division as the Rangers in 2013, their rivalry heated up.

The **2017 Astros** finished the regular season with **101 wins** and 61 losses, the **second-best record** in franchise history.

Where They Play

From 1962 to 1964, the Houston Colt .45s played in Colt Stadium. When the team became the Astros, a new park, called the Astrodome, was built. They played there from 1965 to 1999. Minute Maid Park, which opened in 2000, is their current home. This stadium has a retractable roof, which is perfect for sunny or rainy weather. The total seating capacity for the park is 40,963.

Minute Maid Park's retractable roof is **242 feet** (74 meters) **high**. It takes **12 to 20 minutes** to open or close.

Minute Maid Park has more than 1,400 speakers located throughout the stadium.

Minute Maid
Park

49 24
DIERKER WYNN

42
34
33
25
32 40

AmegyBank
of Texas
The 'A' Bank

Continental
Airlines

PLAY
GREEN
astros.com/playgreen

Methodist
The Methodist
Hospital System

The coyotes wail, along the trail,
deep in the heart of Texas,
The rabbits rush, around the brush,
deep in the heart of Texas.

chron
com
HOUSTON CHRONICLE

Astros   Astros

at&t   at&t   at&t   3:12

C&D SCRAP METAL
WE PAY IN $2 Dollar Bills

KIA KIA MOTORS

FOX SPORTS HO

LEXUS

DeWALT   STANLEY   State Farm

34

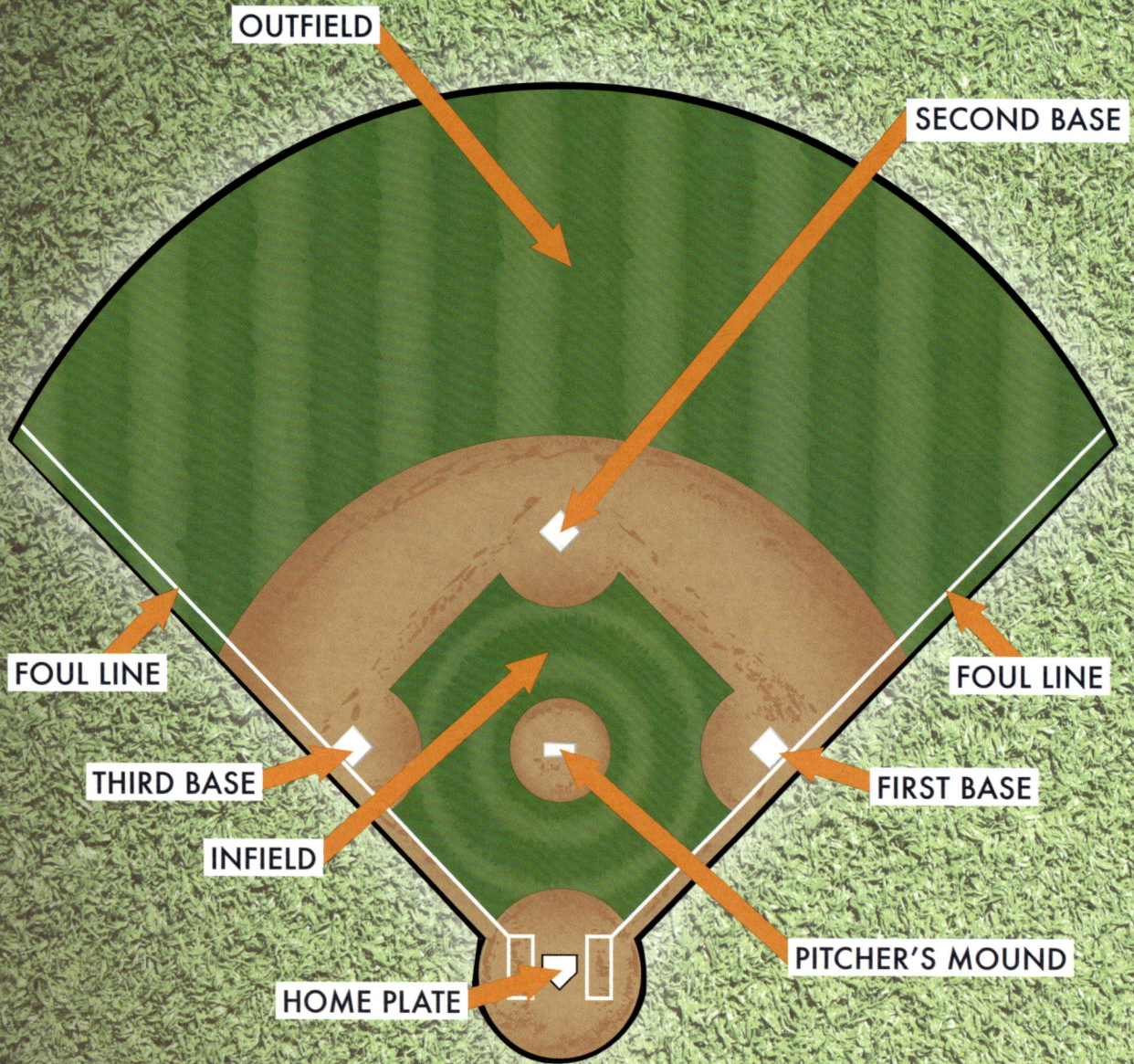

OUTFIELD

SECOND BASE

FOUL LINE

FOUL LINE

THIRD BASE

FIRST BASE

INFIELD

PITCHER'S MOUND

HOME PLATE

THE BASEBALL DIAMOND

Baseball games are played on a field called a diamond. Four bases form this diamond shape. The bases are 90 feet (27 m) apart. The area around and between the bases is called the infield. At the center of the infield is the pitcher's mound. The grass area beyond the bases is called the outfield. White lines start at **home plate** and go toward the outfield. These are the foul lines. Baseballs hit outside these lines are out of play unless a fielder catches them. The outfield walls are about 300–450 feet (91–137 m) from home plate.

Big Days

In the past 55 years, the Astros have had some out-of-this-world seasons. Here are three of the best:

1980: *In a tiebreaker game, Houston defeated the Los Angeles Dodgers and won the National League West Division, advancing to the playoffs for the first time in franchise history. Center fielder César Cedeño logged a .309 batting average that season, along with a whopping 48 stolen bases.*

1998: *The Astros were flying high in 1998, when they set record attendance levels for their home games. The team also finished the season with 102 wins, a franchise best. Second baseman Craig Biggio broke the club record for most runs scored.*

2017: *After more than 10 disappointing years, Houston won their division 21 games ahead of the second-place Los Angeles Angels in 2017. Then, in the biggest game in the team's history, the Astros clinched a World Series win with a 5–1 victory in Game 7 against the Los Angeles Dodgers.*

The Houston Astros finished the 2017 regular season leading the AL for runs, hits, and doubles. Their pitching team was also first in the league, with 1,087 strikeouts.

In a 2013 game, Astros infielder Ronny Cedeño missed a fly ball by a Tampa Bay Rays hitter. The Astros lost the game 0–5.

Tough Days

Like any sports team, the Houston Astros have faced many defeats and disappointments. Here are some of their most difficult seasons:

1979: *Fighting for their first division win, the Astros fell short in 1979. They finished the regular season only one and a half games behind the Cincinnati Reds. The players and their fans were heartbroken.*

1996: *Despite leading their division through most of the 1996 season, the Astros sputtered out in September. That month, they recorded 17 losses and fell out of first place. They finished the season in second place in their division, six games behind the St. Louis Cardinals.*

2013: *During their debut season in the American League, the 2013 Astros struggled to find their footing. The team ended the regular season with a devastating 15-game losing streak. That year, they also set the franchise record for most losses in a season, with 111.*

The Astros' mascot, Orbit, likes to dance. His favorite dance move is the moonwalk.

MEET THE FANS

Usually it is the fans who support their team. After Hurricane Harvey hit Houston in 2017, the opposite happened. The Astros collected food, money, and clothes to support those affected by the disaster. After a week of playing "home" games in Florida, the Astros returned to Minute Maid Park. Orbit, the Astros' fuzzy green spaceman mascot, returned to cheer on his team along with thousands of fans.

In his 13 years with the Astros, José Cruz had 1,937 hits with 138 home runs.

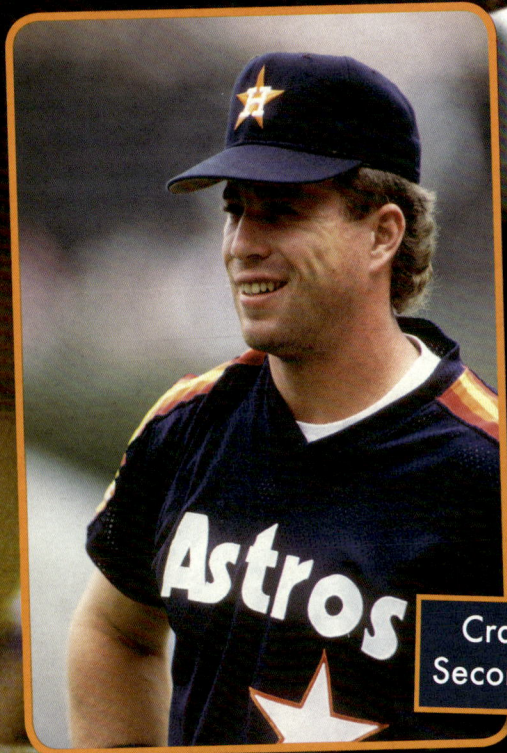

Craig Biggio, Second Baseman

Heroes Then...

The Astros franchise has hosted some incredible talent. During the 1972 and 1973 seasons, César Cedeño stole more than 50 bases and hit more than 20 home runs, setting an MLB record. In the 1970s and 1980s, outfielder José Cruz cranked out hit after hit. He earned multiple team **Most Valuable Player (MVP)** awards and led the National League in hits in 1983. Second baseman Craig Biggio joined the Astros in 1988 and spent his entire 20-year career with them. He was a powerful hitter, finishing his career with more than 3,000 hits, 1,844 runs scored, and 291 home runs. First baseman Jeff Bagwell won the National League Rookie of the Year award in 1991. During his outstanding career, he racked up more than 30 home runs, 100 runs scored, and 100 **runs batted in (RBIs)** in six straight seasons, from 1996 to 2001. He was one of only six players in history to do that.

Heroes Now...

The Houston Astros have assembled one of the best young teams in baseball today. José Altuve, the second baseman, is a league leader in hits and batting average. He has won a **Gold Glove Award**, three **Silver Slugger awards**, and was selected as a player for the **All-Star Game** five times in his seven seasons in the major leagues. Voted American League Rookie of the Year in 2015, shortstop Carlos Correa is a powerful hitter. His .315 batting average in 2017 was the 10th best in the American League. Right fielder George Springer ranked 10th in the American League in triples and home runs in 2017. Pitcher Dallas Keuchel won the **Cy Young Award** in 2015. Another Cy Young Award winner, Justin Verlander, was the 2011 Major League Player of the Year and joined the Astros in late 2017.

The present-day Astros are loaded with star players.

José Altuve, Second Baseman

Carlos Correa, Shortstop

Dallas Keuchel, Pitcher

BAT

BATTING HELMET

BATTING GLOVES

TEAM JERSEY

13

TEAM PANTS

Ronny Cedeño, Infielder

BASEBALL CLEATS

GEARING UP

Baseball players all wear a team jersey and pants. They have to wear a team hat in the field and a helmet when batting. Take a look at Brian McCann and Ronny Cedeño to see some other parts of a baseball player's uniform.

CATCHER'S MASK

CATCHER'S CHEST PROTECTOR

CATCHER'S MITT

Brian McCann, Catcher

CATCHER'S SHIN GUARD

SPORTS STATS

Here are some all-time career records for the Houston Astros. All of the stats are through the 2017 season.

A Major League baseball weighs about **5 ounces** (142 grams). It is **9 inches** (23 cm) around. A leather cover surrounds **hundreds** of feet of string. That string is wound around a small center of **rubber** and **cork**.

Home Runs
Jeff Bagwell, **449**
Lance Berkman, **326**

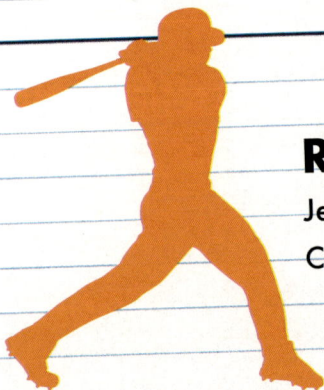

Runs Batted In
Jeff Bagwell, **1,529**
Craig Biggio, **1,175**

Batting Average

Moises Alou, **.331**

José Altuve, **.316**

Stolen Bases

César Cedeño, **487**

Craig Biggio, **414**

Wins by a Pitcher

Joe Niekro, **144**

Roy Oswalt, **143**

Wins by a Manager

Bill Virdon, **544**

Larry Dierker, **435**

Earned Run Average

Roger Clemens, **2.40**

Joe Sambito, **2.42**

Quiz

1 In which division do the Astros play?

2 What was the Astros' original team name?

3 What is the name of the Astros' current stadium?

4 Which team did the Astros beat to win the 2017 World Series?

5 What is the name of the Astros' mascot?

6 Which Astros pitcher won the Cy Young Award in 2015?

7 How much does a baseball weigh?

8 Which Astros player has had the most home runs?

Answers

1. The West Division of the American League
2. The Houston Colt .45s
3. Minute Maid Park
4. The Los Angeles Dodgers
5. Orbit
6. Dallas Keuchel
7. About 5 ounces (142 g)
8. Jeff Bagwell

Key Words

All-Star Game: an annual midseason game in which the best players from the AL and NL play against each other

Cy Young Award: an annual award given to the best pitcher in each league

divisions: groups of teams that form one part of a professional sports league

franchise: a team that belongs to a professional sports league

Gold Glove Award: an annual award given to a player from each defensive position in each league

home plate: the base where a batter stands and where a runner must touch to score a run

Most Valuable Player (MVP): an annual award given to one player from each league

rivals: teams that have a strong sense of competition with each other

runs batted in (RBIs): when a batter makes a hit or is walked, causing another player to score

Silver Slugger awards: annual awards given to a player from each offensive position of each league

wild card: a team, other than the top teams, that also qualifies for the playoffs

World Series: an annual series played between the champions of each league

Index

Altuve, José 6, 24, 25, 29

American League (AL) 7, 8, 11, 17, 19, 24, 30

Bagwell, Jeff 23, 28, 30

Biggio, Craig 16, 22, 23, 28, 29

Cedeño, César 16, 23, 29

Cedeño, Ronny 18, 26, 27

Colt Stadium 12

Correa, Carlos 24, 25

Cruz, José 22, 23

field diagram 14

Houston Colt .45s 8, 12, 30

Hurricane Harvey 21

Keuchel, Dallas 24, 25, 30

Major League Baseball (MLB) 7, 11, 23

McCann, Brian 27

Minute Maid Park 4, 12, 13, 21, 30

National League (NL) 7, 8, 16, 23

Orbit 20, 21, 30

playoffs 7, 16

Texas Rangers 11

Verlander, Justin 24

World Series 4, 5, 16, 30

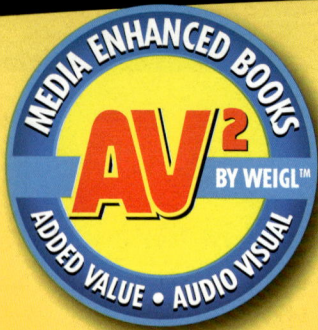

Log on to www.av2books.com

AV² by Weigl brings you media enhanced books that support active learning. Go to www.av2books.com, and enter the special code found on page 2 of this book. You will gain access to enriched and enhanced content that supplements and complements this book. Content includes video, audio, weblinks, quizzes, a slide show, and activities.

AV² Online Navigation

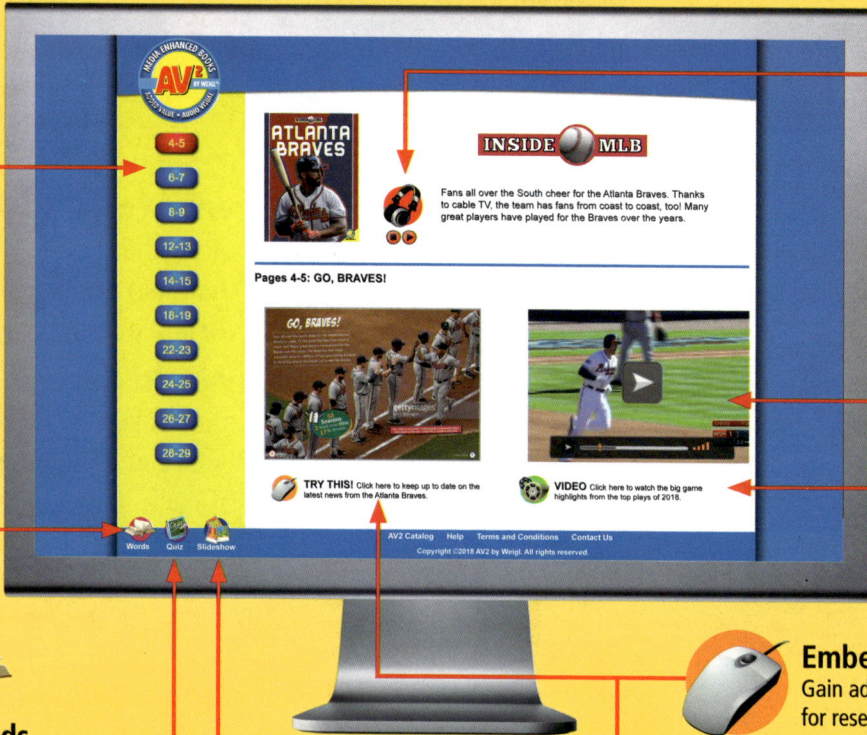

Audio
Listen to sections of the book read aloud

Book Pages
AV² pages directly correspond to pages in the book.

Video
Watch informative video clips.

Key Words
Study vocabulary, and complete a matching word activity.

Embedded Weblinks
Gain additional information for research.

Quizzes
Test your knowledge.

Slide Show
View images and captions, and prepare a presentation.

Try This!
Complete activities and hands-on experiments.

AV² was built to bridge the gap between print and digital. We encourage you to tell us what you like and what you want to see in the future.

Sign up to be an AV² Ambassador at www.av2books.com/ambassador.

Due to the dynamic nature of the Internet, some of the URLs and activities provided as part of AV² by Weigl may have changed or ceased to exist. AV² by Weigl accepts no responsibility for any such changes. All media enhanced books are regularly monitored to update addresses and sites in a timely manner. Contact AV² by Weigl at 1-866-649-3445 or av2books@weigl.com with any questions, comments, or feedback.